Frank Schaffer Publications®

GRADE 2

# Spanish

# Frank Schaffer Publications®

Printed in the United States of America. All rights reserved. Limited Reproduction Permission: Permission to duplicate these materials is limited to the person for whom they are purchased. Reproduction for an entire school or school district is unlawful and strictly prohibited. Frank Schaffer Publications is an imprint of School Specialty Publishing. Copyright © 2006 School Specialty Publishing.

Send all inquiries to:
Frank Schaffer Publications
3195 Wilson Drive NW
Grand Rapids, Michigan 49534

*Spanish*—Grade 2

ISBN 0-7696-8242-1

1 2 3 4 5 6 7 8 9 10 WAL 10 09 08 07 06

# Table of Contents

# Numbers 0–10

Trace, then write each of the number words from 0 to 10 in Spanish.
Use the words at the left to help you.

0    cero     cero

1    uno     uno

2    dos     dos

3    tres     tres

4    cuatro     cuatro

5    cinco     cinco

6    seis     seis

7    siete     siete

8    ocho     ocho

9    nueve     nueve

10    diez     diez

# Numbers 0–10

Say each word out loud. Circle the number that tells the meaning of the word.

| seis | 5 | 0 | 6 |
| cho | 1 | 9 | 8 |
| uno | 3 | 1 | 8 |
| cero | 8 | 10 | 0 |
| siete | 9 | 7 | 1 |
| tres | 0 | 3 | 5 |
| diez | 10 | 8 | 7 |
| nueve | 4 | 2 | 9 |
| cuatro | 7 | 5 | 4 |
| dos | 2 | 6 | 3 |
| cinco | 6 | 4 | 5 |

# Dot-to-Dot

Connect the dots. Start with the Spanish word for one and stop at ten. What shape did you get? _____

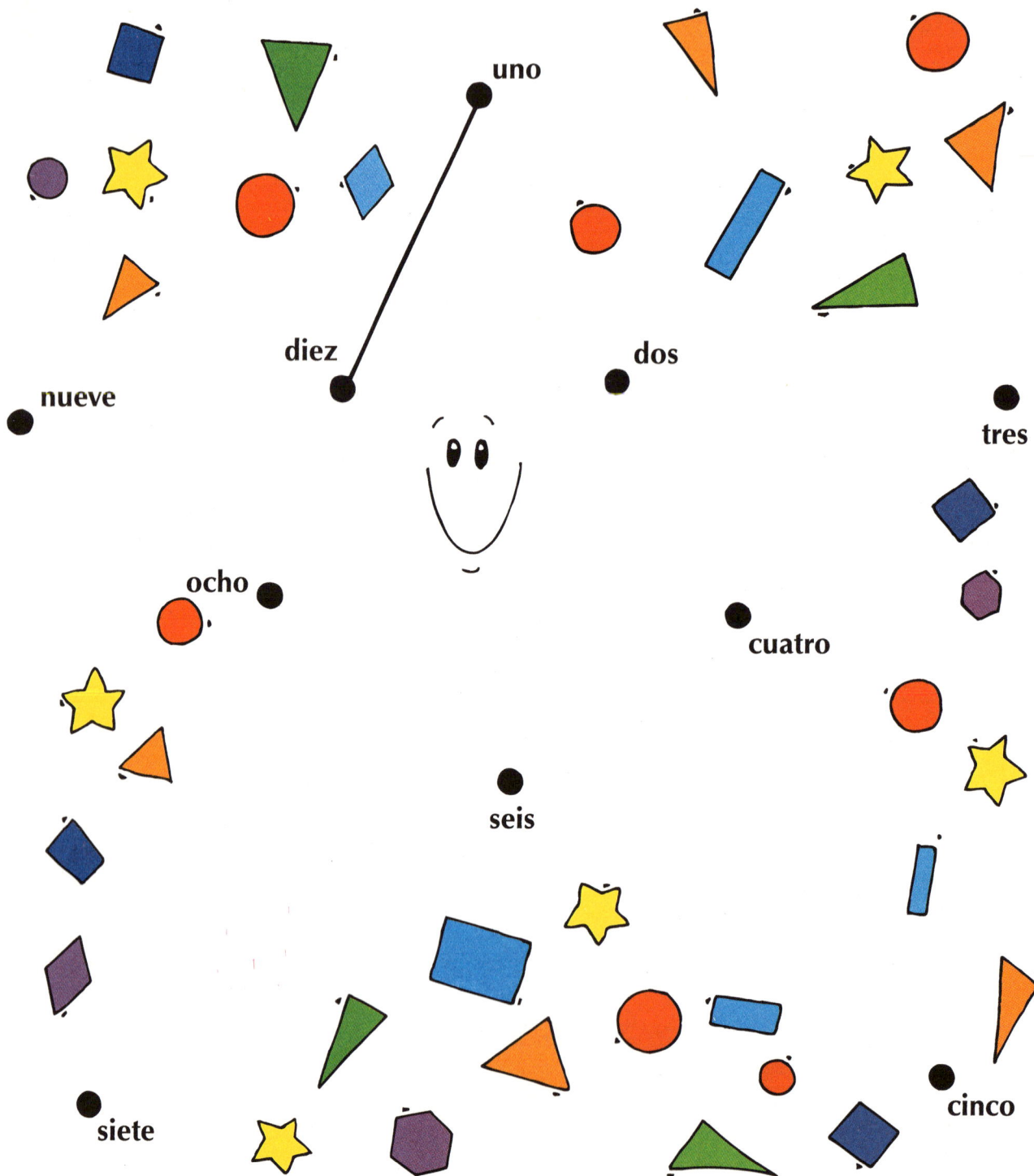

uno

diez

nueve

dos

tres

ocho

cuatro

seis

cinco

siete

# Numbers 0–20

In the left column, write the number words from 0 to 10 in Spanish. Use the words in the box below to help you. Then, in the second column, write the numbers beside each Spanish word. Examples are done for you.

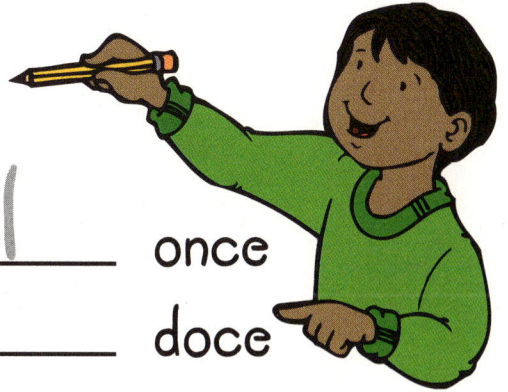

0   cero _____

1   _____

2   _____

3   _____

4   _____

5   _____

6   _____

7   _____

8   _____

9   _____

10  _____

___11___  once

_____  doce

_____  trece

_____  catorce

_____  quince

_____  dieciséis

_____  diecisiete

_____  dieciocho

_____  diecinueve

_____  veinte

| siete | ocho | uno | seis | nueve |
|-------|------|-----|------|-------|
| cero  | cinco | dos | cuatro | diez | tres |

Now, count from 1 to 20 in Spanish. Point to the numbers as you say them.

1  2  3  4  5  6  7  8  9  10
11  12  13  14  15  16  17  18  19  20

# Show Your Numbers

In each box, write the number for the word written. Then, draw and color pictures that show the numbers.

**dieciséis** means

**trece** means

**ocho** means

**catorce** means

**seis** means

**once** means

**dos** means

**veinte** means

**cinco** means

**doce** means

**diez** means

**quince** means

# Sunshine 0–20

Write the number for each Spanish word. Cross out the correct number of suns to show the number written in Spanish. The first is done for you.

quince __15__

veinte _____

tres _____

once _____

nueve _____

trece _____

catorce _____

dieciocho _____

cero _____

doce _____

My favorite number

_____

seis _____

Name _____

# Number Puzzle

Write the English number words in the puzzle spaces. Follow the Spanish clues.

## Word Bank

| | | | |
|---|---|---|---|
| one | eight | eleven | seventeen |
| two | nine | thirteen | eighteen |
| six | ten | fourteen | twenty |

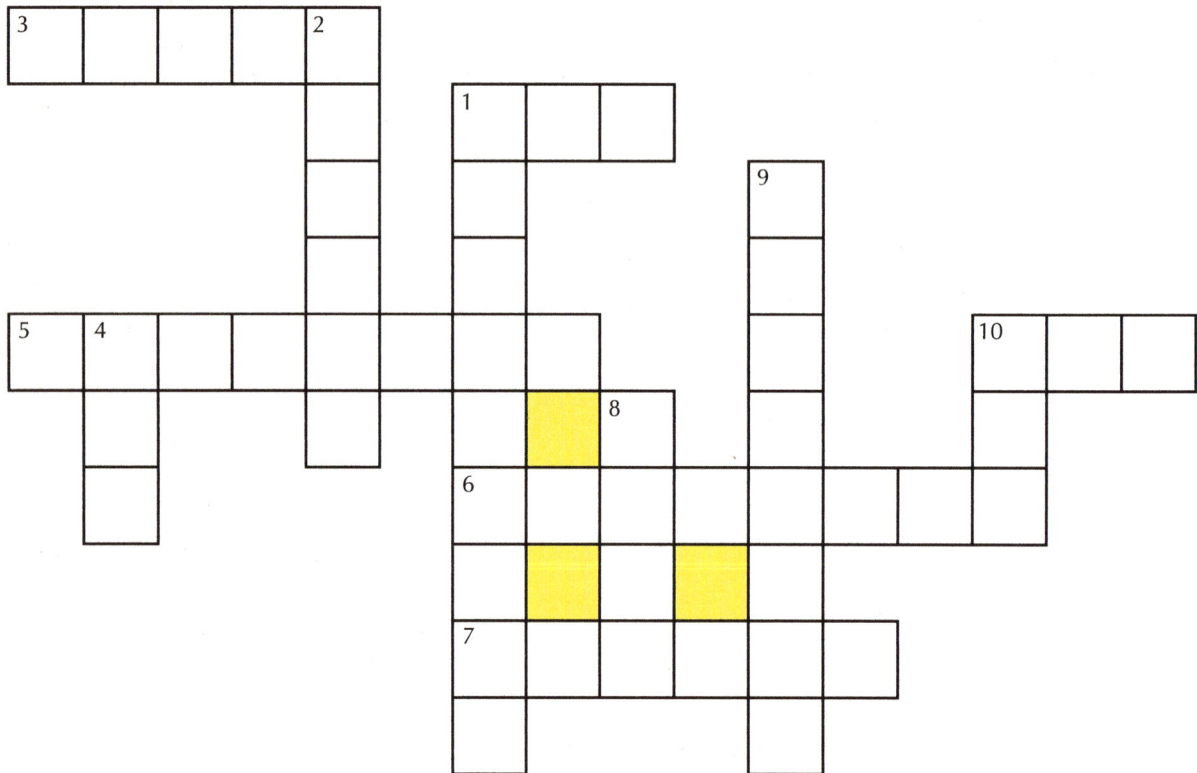

## Down

1. diecisiete
2. veinte
4. uno
8. nueve
9. dieciocho
10. diez

## Across

1. seis
3. ocho
5. catorce
6. trece
7. once
10. dos

# Counting On

Follow a pattern to write the numbers from 21–29. Change *veinte* (20) to *veinti* and add the number words from *uno* to *nueve*. (Watch for accent marks on *dos, tres,* and *seis.*)

Rewrite the number words in the Word Bank in order.

## Word Bank

| | | | |
|---|---|---|---|
| veintiséis | veinticinco | treinta | veintiocho |
| veintidós | veintiuno | veintinueve | veinticuatro |
| | veintisiete | veintitrés | |

21 _____     26 _____

22 _____     27 _____

23 _____     28 _____

24 _____     29 _____

25 _____     30 _____

Complete the pattern to write the numbers from 31–39. Use the word *y* to join *treinta* (30) with the number words *uno* to *nueve.*

30 _____     35 _____

31 _____     36 _____

32 _____     37 _____

33 _____     38 _____

34 _____     39 _____

# The Alphabet

## El abecedario (the alphabet)

| | | | | | |
|---|---|---|---|---|---|
| **a** | a | **k** | ka | **s** | ese |
| **b** | be | **l** | ele | **t** | te |
| **c** | ce | **m** | eme | **u** | u |
| **d** | de | **n** | ene | **v** | ve |
| **e** | e | **ñ** | eñe | **w** | doble ve |
| **f** | efe | **o** | o | **x** | equis |
| **g** | ge | **p** | pe | **y** | i griega |
| **h** | hache | **q** | cu | **z** | zeta |
| **i** | i | **r** | ere | | |
| **j** | jota | **rr** | erre | | |

## Listening Practice

Write the Spanish word for each number below. Then, spell each word out loud.

| | | | |
|---|---|---|---|
| 1 _____ | 5 _____ | 9 _____ | 13 _____ |
| 2 _____ | 6 _____ | 10 _____ | 14 _____ |
| 3 _____ | 7 _____ | 11 _____ | 15 _____ |
| 4 _____ | 8 _____ | 12 _____ | 16 _____ |

 *Spanish: Grade 2*

# Using You

Spanish uses two different forms of the pronoun *you*.

**Tú** is used when talking to

**tú**

1. someone you refer to by a first name.
2. your sister, brother, or cousin.
3. a classmate.
4. a close friend.
5. a child younger than yourself.

**Usted** (**Ud.**) is used when talking to

**usted**

1. someone with a title.
2. an older person.
3. a stranger.
4. a person of authority.

Write the names of 6 or more people in each box below.

| Use **tú** when you are talking to . . . | Use **usted** when you are talking to . . . |
|---|---|
|  |  |

# Picking Pronouns

Spanish uses two different forms of the pronoun *you*.

**Tú** is used when talking to

1. someone you refer to by a first name.
2. your sister, brother, or cousin.
3. a classmate.
4. a close friend.
5. a child younger than yourself.

## tú

**Usted** (**Ud.**) is used when talking to

1. someone with a title.
2. an older person.
3. a stranger.
4. a person of authority.

## usted

Explain to whom you might be talking and what you are asking in each question.

¿Cómo te llamas tú? _____

¿Cómo se llama usted? _____

¿Cómo estás tú? _____

¿Cómo está usted? _____

¿Cuántos años tienes tú? _____

¿Cuántos años tiene usted? _____

# More Than One

Spanish nouns can be placed into two groups—singular nouns (one of something) or plural nouns (more than one of something). Nouns that end in –s are usually plural. Nouns ending in other letters are usually singular.

Read the following familiar nouns. Write **S** if the noun is singular and **P** if the noun is plural.

_____ 1. calcetines     _____ 2. dedo     _____ 3. botas

_____ 4. cuerpo     _____ 5. vegetales     _____ 6. ciudad

_____ 7. escuela     _____ 8. sandalias     _____ 9. zapatos

_____ 10. guantes     _____ 11. casa     _____ 12. boca

Follow these rules to write the following Spanish words in the plural.

1. If the word ends in a vowel, add -s.
2. If the word ends in a consonant, add -es.
3. If the word ends in z, change the z to c before adding -es.

1. carne _____     6. nariz _____

2. silla _____     7. abrigo _____

3. ciudad _____     8. señor _____

4. lápiz _____     9. borrador _____

5. azul _____     10. pollo _____

# More and More

Write the plural form of each Spanish clue word in the puzzle.

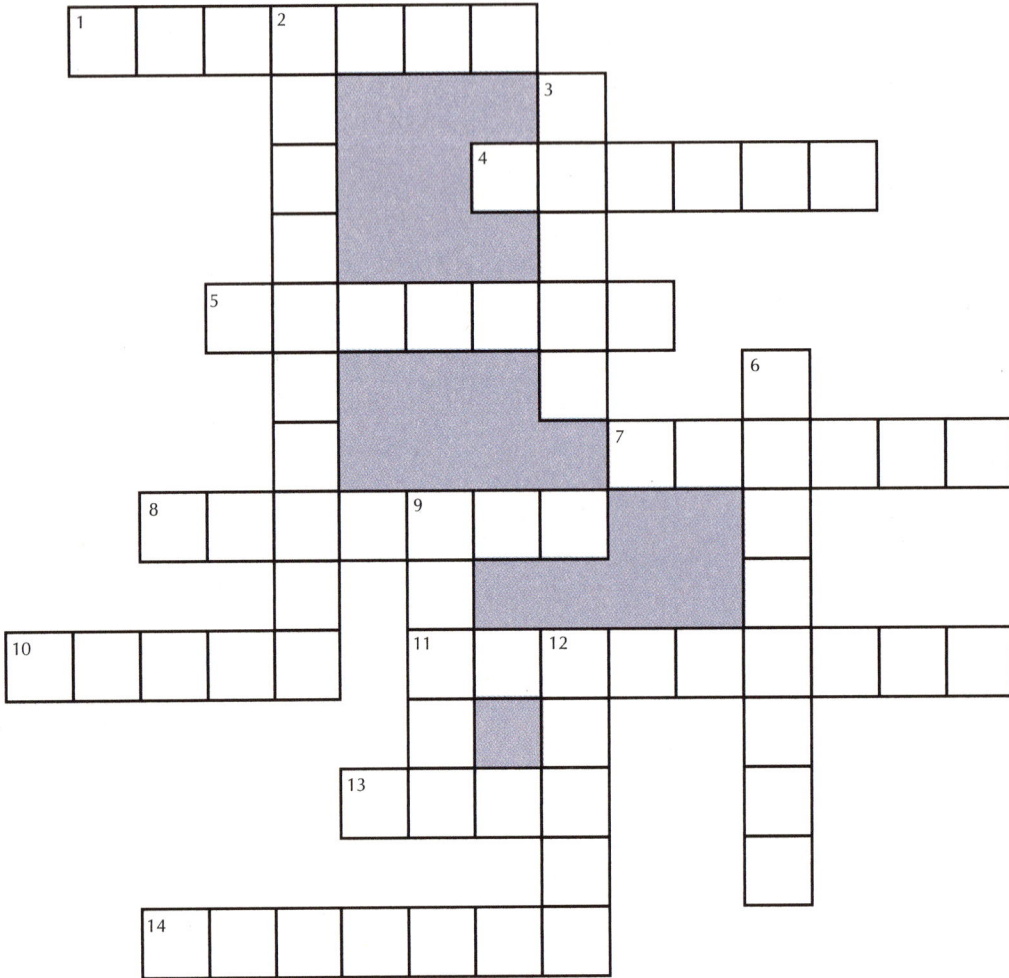

## Across

1. hombro
4. falda
5. zapato
7. museo
8. nariz
10. gato
11. sombrero
13. oso
14. lápiz

## Down

2. borrador
3. vaso
6. escuela
9. casa
12. mesa

Name _____

# First Sentences

Create original sentences in Spanish using these sentence starters and the verbs in the Word Bank. You may use one sentence starter more than once. Write the English meanings on the lines below the Spanish.

### Word Bank

| comer | beber | dormir | tocar |
|-------|-------|--------|-------|
| hablar | limpiar | mirar | dar |

### Sentence Starters

Me gusta _____ .          (I like _____ .)

No me gusta _____ .          (I don't like _____ .)

Quiero _____ .          (I want _____ .)

Necesito _____ .          (I need _____ .)

1. _____

_____

2. _____

_____

3. _____

_____

4. _____

_____

5. _____

_____

# Action Words

Refer to the Word Bank to write the Spanish word that matches each picture.

| Word Bank | comer | estudiar | limpiar | mirar | jugar | dar |
|---|---|---|---|---|---|---|
| | hablar | beber | dormir | trabajar | tocar | ir |

to clean

to touch

to eat

to speak

hablar

to watch

to drink

to give

to sleep

to study

to go

to work

to play

18

*Spanish: Grade 2*

# Capitals

Spanish uses capital letters less often than the English language. Follow these rules as your guide.

### Capitalization Rules

1. All Spanish sentences begin with capital letters.

2. Names of people begin with capital letters.

3. Names of places (cities, regions, countries, continents) and holidays begin with capital letters.

4. Titles are not capitalized unless abbreviated (*señor–Sr., usted–Ud.*).

5. Some words that are normally capitalized in English may not be capitalized in Spanish (nationalities, religions, languages, months, and days).

Write *sí* if the word should be capitalized. Write *no* if it should remain lowercase.

1. sarah _____

2. inglés _____

3. navidad _____

4. español _____

5. mexicano _____

6. africa _____

7. señor _____

8. enero _____

9. domingo _____

10. católico _____

11. santa fé _____

12. viernes _____

13. méxico _____

14. julio _____

15. colorado _____

16. miguel _____

# Categories

Read the list of words given. Write the words in the proper columns. If the word needs a capital letter, write it that way.

| | | | | |
|---|---|---|---|---|
| los angeles | españa | ustedes | americano | lunes |
| maría | susana | san antonio | américa del norte | méxico |
| uds. | sr. | santa fé | español | católico |
| inglés | sra. | oceano pacífico | señora | señor |
| san diego | viernes | juan | josé | |
| señorita | cuba | septiembre | mexicano | |

| People | Places | Titles | Not Capitalized |
|---|---|---|---|
| | | | |
| | | | |
| | | | |
| | | | |
| | | | |
| | | | |
| | | | |
| | | | |
| | | | |
| | | | |
| | | | |
| | | | |

# Polite Words

Say each Spanish expression out loud.

| | | |
|---|---|---|
| **¿Cuántos años tienes?** |  | How old are you? |
| **Tengo seis años.** |  | I am six years old. |
| **por favor** |  | please |
| **gracias** |  | thank you |

| | | | | |
|---|---|---|---|---|
| **amigo** |  friend | **amiga** | friend |

| | | | | |
|---|---|---|---|---|
| **sí** ✓ | **no** ⊘ | **amigos** |  friends |

| | | |
|---|---|---|
| **¡Hasta luego!** |  | See you later! |

*Spanish: Grade 2*

# Introductions

Say each expression out loud. Circle the picture that tells the meaning of each word.

| gracias |  | ✓ |  |

| Tengo seis años. |  |  | |

| por favor | | |  |

| amigo | | | |

| amigos | ⊘ |  |  |

| ¡Hasta luego! |  |  |  |

| amiga | |  |  |

| sí | ⊘ | ✓ |  |

# Puzzle of the Week

Write the Spanish words in the puzzle.

## Across

2. Thursday
7. Wednesday

## Down

1. Monday
3. Saturday
4. Friday
5. Sunday
6. Tuesday

## Word Bank

jueves     domingo     martes

sábado     viernes     lunes

miércoles

# Spanish Months

Write the Spanish word for the clue words in the crossword puzzle.

## Across

4. July
9. May
10. September
11. June
12. January

## Down

1. April
2. November
3. December
5. March
6. February
7. August
8. October

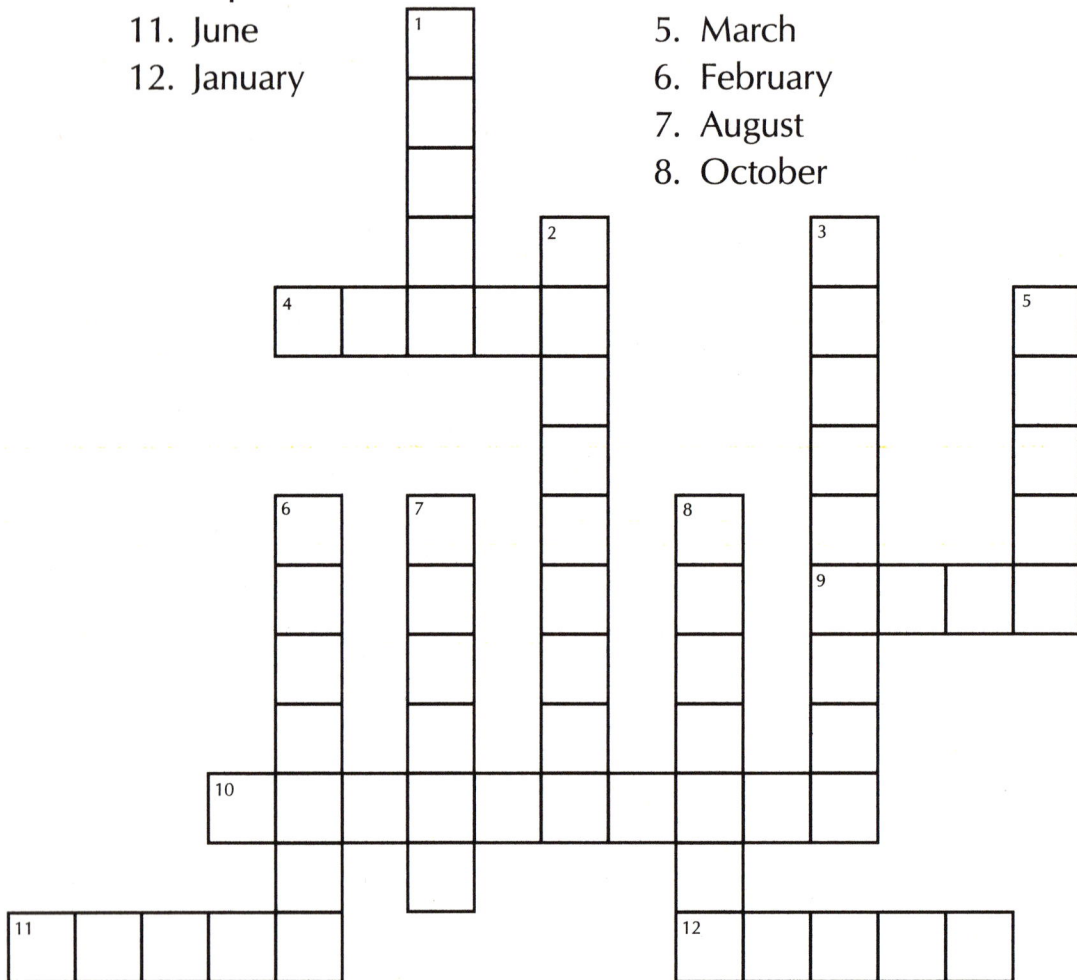

## Word Bank

| | | | |
|---|---|---|---|
| marzo | mayo | diciembre | junio |
| septiembre | octubre | julio | agosto |
| abril | enero | febrero | noviembre |

# Pictures to Color

Color the pictures according to each color word.

## rojo

## azul

## verde

## anaranjado

## morado

## amarillo

 *Spanish: Grade 2*

# Rainbow Colors

Color the picture according to the color words shown.

rojo

anaranjado

amarillo

verde

azul

morado

# Color the Cars

Color the cars according to the color words shown.

rojo

azul

verde

morado

anaranjado

amarillo

# Color Copy

Copy the following words in the color of each word.
Which word is hard to see with the actual color? _____

rojo

azul

verde

anaranjado

morado

amarillo

café

negro

blanco

rosado

# Food Meanings

Say each word out loud. Circle the picture that shows the meaning of each word.

| papa |  |  |
| --- | --- | --- |
| ensalada |  | 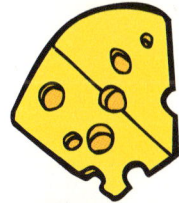 |
| queso | 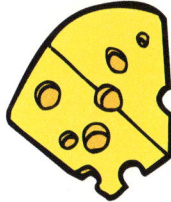 |  |
| pan |  | 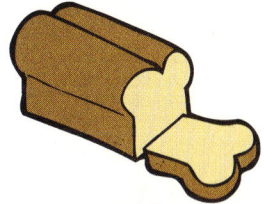 |
| leche |  |  |
| pollo |  | 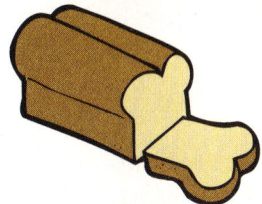 |
| jugo |  |  |

# Mixed-Up Food

Draw a line from the word to the food picture.

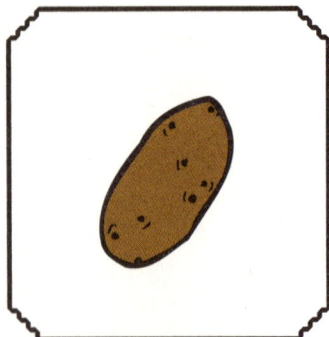

papa

ensalada

queso

pan

leche

jugo

pollo

# Food Words

Say each word out loud. Copy each word and color the picture.

**sopa**

**agua**

**naranja**

**carne**

**plátano**

**manzana**

**sandwich**

# Animals All Around

Copy each word and color the pictures.

_____

- - - - - - - - - - - - - - - - - - -

_____

_____

- - - - - - - - - - - - - - - - - - -

_____

▶ perro

▶ gato

▶ pájaro

▶ pez

▶ pato

▶ culebra

- - - - - - - - - - - - - - - - - - -

_____

_____

- - - - - - - - - - - - - - - - - - -

_____

# Animal Art

Choose four animals and draw each animal in its home. Label it with the Spanish animal word.

# Clothing

Say each word out loud. Copy each word and color the picture.

pantalones

gorro

vestido

camisa

zapatos

calcetines

# Clothing

Say each word out loud. Copy each word and color the picture.

abrigo

chaqueta

falda

guantes

botas

pantalones cortos

# Remember These?

Fill in the blanks with the missing letters. Use the Spanish clothing words at the bottom to help you.

c _ _ _ _ a

f _ _ _ _ _

a
l
z _ _ _ _ _
c
e
p _ _ _ _ _ _ _ _ _
t
i
v _ _ _ _ _ _
n
e
s

g _ _ _ _

b

| camisa | vestido | pantalones | falda |
| zapatos | gorro | abrigo | botas |

# What Belongs?

Circle the item that does not belong with the other two. Write its name in Spanish below its picture.

Circle the two items that are alike. Say the item in Spanish that is not like the other two. Color the pictures.

# Head to Toe

Using the Word Banks, label the parts of the face and body.

## Word Bank

cara    ojos    boca    nariz    dientes    orejas    pelo

## Word Bank

| cuerpo | cabeza | mano | pierna | hombro |
|--------|--------|------|--------|--------|
| brazo | dedo | pie | rodilla | estómago |

# Head and Shoulders

Refer to the Word Bank to label each body part in Spanish.

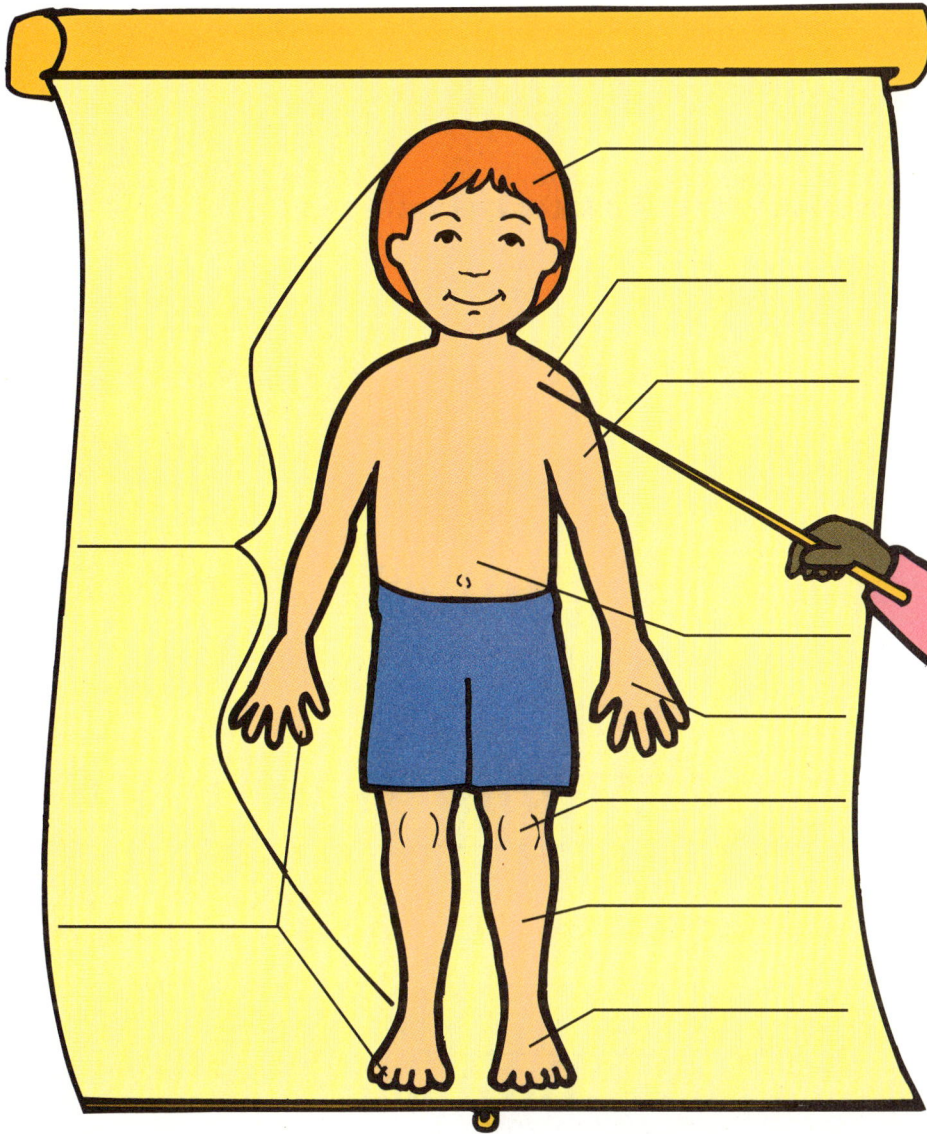

## Word Bank

| | |
|---|---|
| cuerpo | pie |
| brazo | pierna |
| cabeza | rodilla |
| dedo | hombro |
| mano | estómago |

**39**

*Spanish: Grade 2*

**Name** _____

# Knees and Toes

Write the Spanish words for the clues in the crossword puzzle.

## Word Bank
cuerpo   cabeza   mano   pierna   hombro
brazo    dedo     pie    rodilla  estómago

## Across

2. foot
3. body
5. knee
6. head
7. shoulder
9. hand

## Down

1. finger or toe
2. leg
4. stomach
8. arm

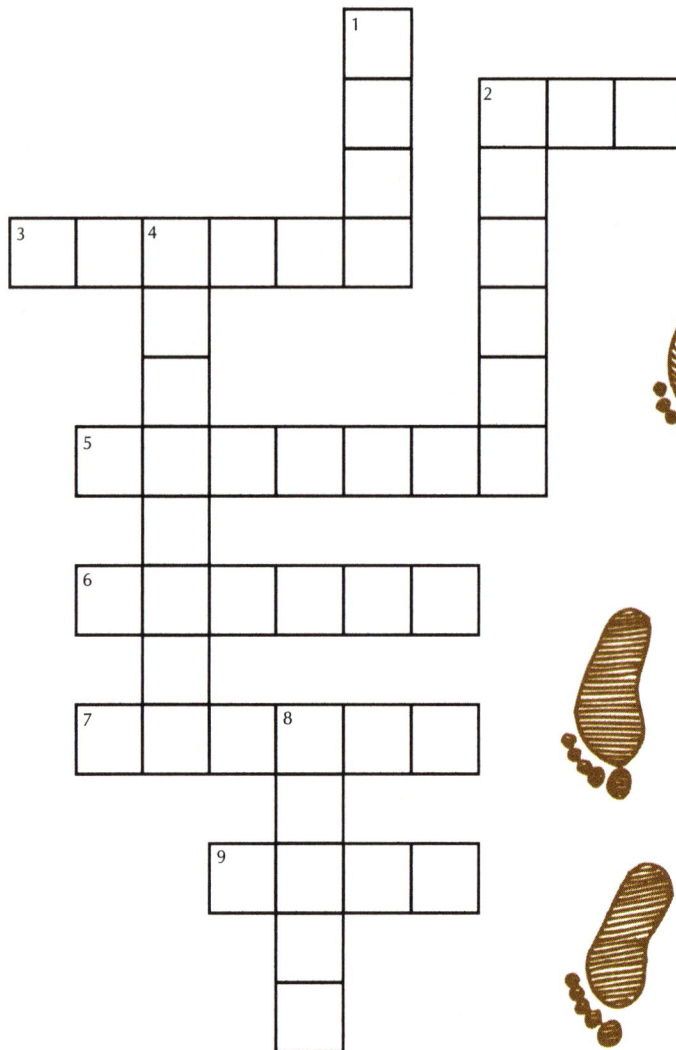

*Spanish: Grade 2*

# Family Word Meanings

Say each word out loud. Circle the picture that shows the meaning of each word.

| | | |
|---|---|---|
| **padre** |  |  |
| **chica** |  |  |
| **abuela** |  |  |
| **madre** |  |  |
| **abuelo** |  |  |
| **chico** |  |  |

# Family

Copy each word and color the pictures.

-------------------------------------

▶ madre

-------------------------------------

▶ padre

-------------------------------------

▶ abuelo

◀ abuela

-------------------------------------

▶ chica

▶ chico

Let's learn two new words:

▶ hermano

▶ hermana

*Spanish: Grade 2*

Name _____

# Family Crossword

Use the Spanish words at the bottom of the page to fill in your answers.

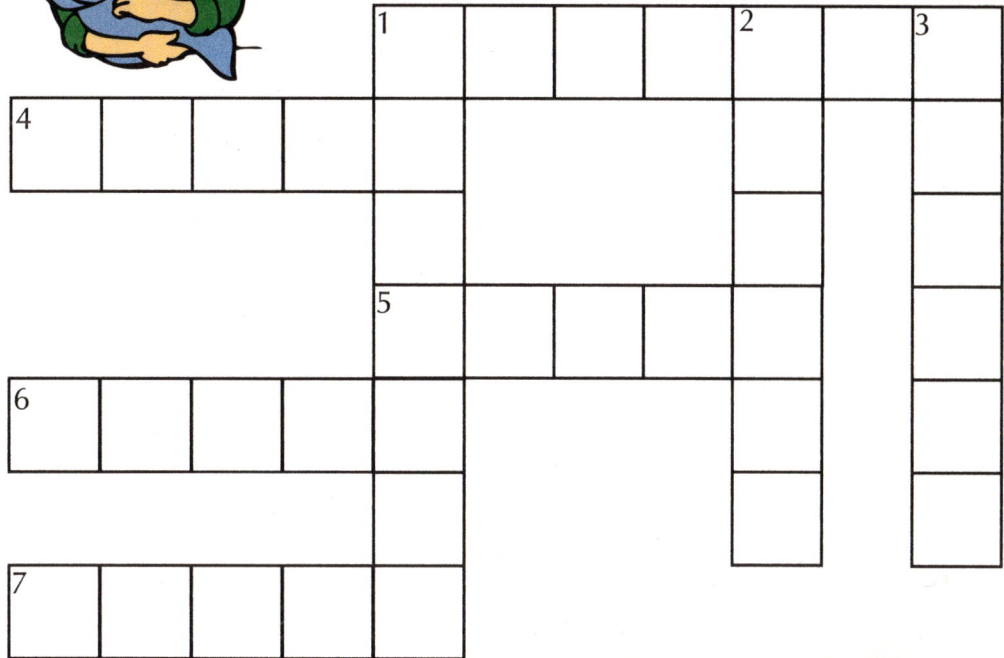

## ACROSS

**1.** sister
**4.** father
**5.** mother
**6.** girl
**7.** boy

## DOWN

**1.** brother
**2.** grandmother
**3.** grandfather

| padre | madre |
|-------|-------|
| chico | chica |
| abuelo | abuela |
| hermano | hermana |

*Spanish: Grade 2*

**Name** _____

# Listen Well

Say each word out loud. Circle the picture for each Spanish word.

| padre | | | |
|---|---|---|---|
| abuelo | | | |
| hermana | | | |
| chica | | | |
| abuela | | | |
| madre | | | |
| hermano | | | |
| chico | | | |

*Spanish: Grade 2*

# My Neighborhood

Draw a picture of an imaginary neighborhood. Add streets, trees, and whatever else you wish to make your neighborhood look nice. Color your picture.

## Mi barrio

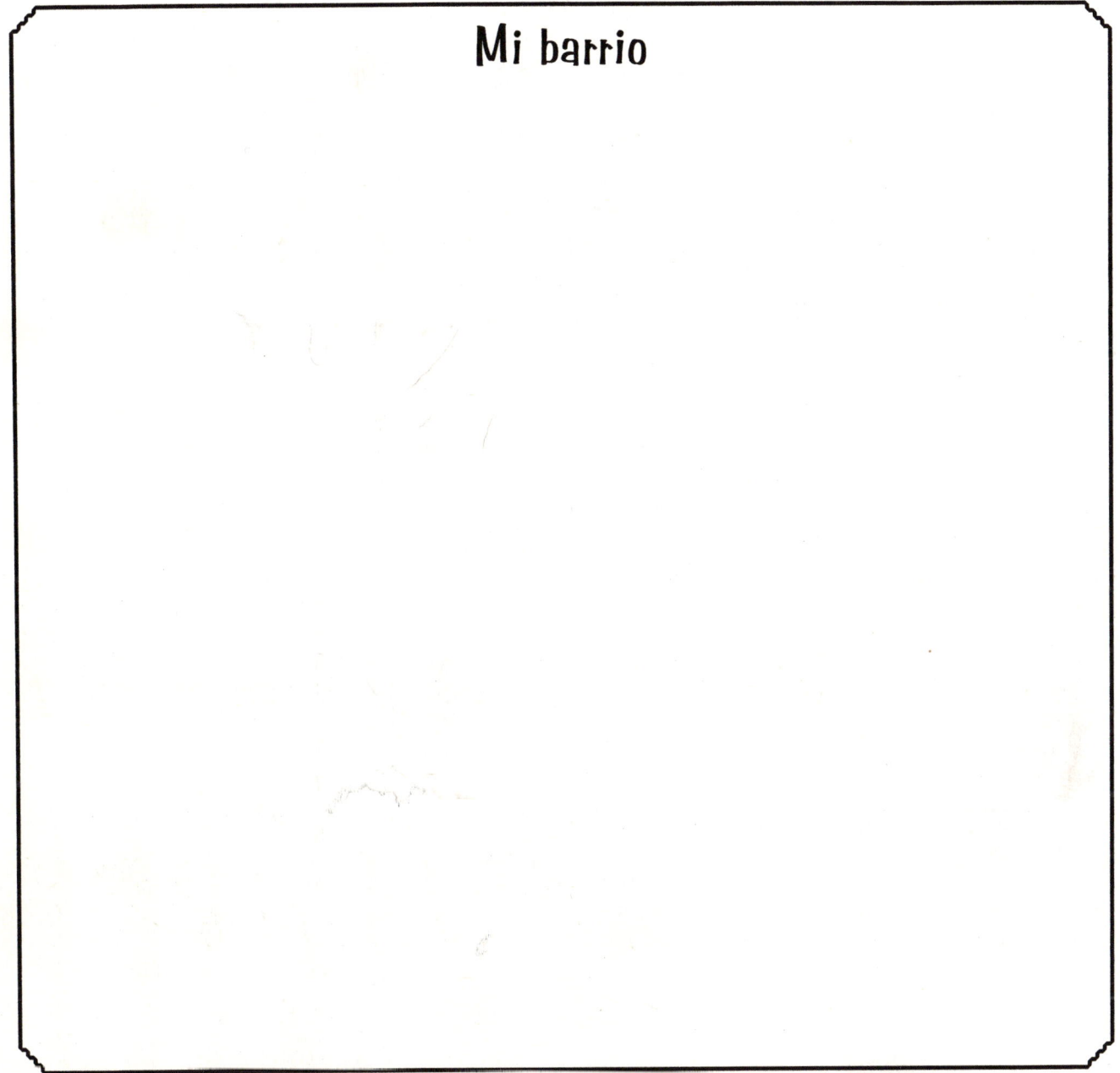

Label your neighborhood with the words you learned.

casa    parque    biblioteca    tienda    escuela    museo

Name _____

# Picture This

Say each word out loud. Circle the picture that shows the meaning of each word.

| casa |  |  |
| escuela |  |  |
| tienda |  |  |
| parque |  |  |
| biblioteca |  |  |
| museo |  |  |

*Spanish: Grade 2*

# Places to Go

Say each word out loud. Copy each word and color the picture.

_____
- - - - - - - - - - - - - - - - - - - - - -
_____

▶ **museo**

_____
- - - - - - - - - - - - - - - - - - - - - -
_____

▶ **escuela**

▶ **casa**

Dinosaurios

▶ **tienda**

▶ **parque**

FOOD-MART

▶ **biblioteca**

_____
- - - - - - - - - - - - - - - - - - - - - -
_____

# Place Words

Fill in the blanks for place words. Use the Spanish words at the bottom to help you.

t

**b i b l i o t e c a**

m

p

c

| escuela | museo | casa |
|---------|-------|------|
| biblioteca | tienda | parque |

# Classroom Things

Copy each word and color the picture.

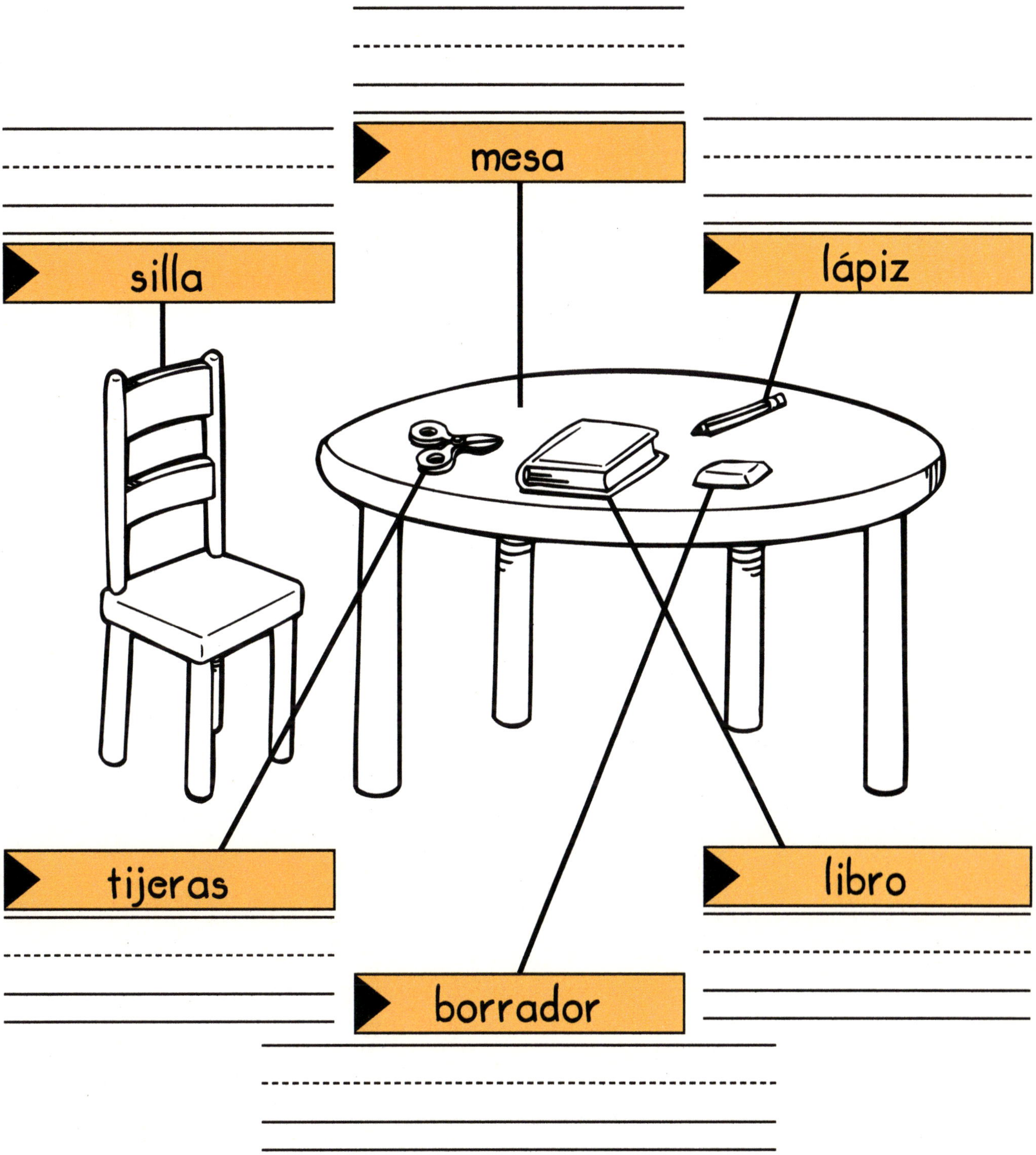

_____
- - - - - - - - - - - - - - - - - - - - - - -
_____

▶ **mesa**

_____
- - - - - - - - - - - - - - - - - - - - - - -
_____

▶ **silla**

_____
- - - - - - - - - - - - - - - - - - - - - - -
_____

▶ **lápiz**

▶ **tijeras**

▶ **libro**

- - - - - - - - - - - - - - - - - - - - - - -
_____
_____

▶ **borrador**

_____
- - - - - - - - - - - - - - - - - - - - - - -
_____

# Classroom Words

Say each word out loud. Copy each word and color the picture.

cuaderno

ventana

puerta

pluma

papel

escritorio

**50**

*Spanish: Grade 2*

**Name** _____

# Listen Carefully

Say each word out loud. Circle the picture that tells the meaning of each word.

| | | | |
|---|---|---|---|
| **libro** |  |  |  |
| **tijeras** |  | | |
| **ventana** | | | |
| **silla** | | | |
| **pluma** | | |  |
| **lápiz** | | | |
| **cuaderno** | | |  |
| **mesa** | | | |
| **puerta** |  | |  |

*Spanish: Grade 2*

# Songs and Chants

## Diez (veinte) amigos

(to the tune of "Ten Little Fingers")

*Uno, dos, tres amigos,*
*cuatro, cinco, seis amigos,*
*siete, ocho, nueve amigos,*
*diez amigos son.*

*Diez, nueve, ocho amigos*
*siete, seis, cinco amigos*
*cuatro, tres, dos amigos,*
*un amigo es.*

*Once, doce, trece amigos,*
*catorce, quince, dieciséis amigos,*
*diecisiete, dieciocho,*
*diecinueve amigos,*
*veinte amigos son.*

## Community Song

(to the tune of "Here We Go 'Round the Mulberry Bush")

*Escuela* is school,
*museo* — museum,
*casa* is house,
*tienda* is store,
*biblioteca* is library,
*parque* is the park for me!

*Spanish: Grade 2*

# Songs and Chants

### Family Song

(to the tune of "Are You Sleeping?")

*Padre* — father,
*madre* — mother,
*chico* — boy,
*chica* — girl,
*abuelo* is grandpa,
*abuela* is grandma.
Our family, our family.

*Hermano* — brother,
*hermana* — sister,
*chico* — boy,
*chica* — girl,
*padre y madre*,
*abuelo y abuela*.
Our family, our family.

### Los días de la semana

(to the tune of "Clementine")

Domingo, lunes,
martes, miércoles,
jueves, viernes, sábado,
domingo, lunes,
martes, miércoles,
jueves, viernes, sábado. *(Repitan)*

*Spanish: Grade 2*

# Chants

## Body Chant

Cabeza, hombros, rodillas, dedos, rodillas, dedos, rodillas, dedos
Cabeza, hombros, rodillas, dedos
Ojos, orejas, boca, nariz.

## Number Chant

*Dos y dos son cuatro, cuatro y dos son seis, seis y dos son ocho, y ocho más, dieciséis.*
(Two and two are four, four and two are six, six and two are eight, and eight more, sixteen.)

## Clothing Chant

| | |
|---|---|
| *Abrigo rosado, vestido blanco,* | Pink coat, white dress, |
| *camisa café, sombrero morado,* | brown shirt, purple hat, |
| *blusas verdes, pantalones rojos,* | green blouses, red pants, |
| *botas azules, zapatos negros.* | blue boots, black shoes. |

## Adjective Chant

| | |
|---|---|
| *La casa es grande, la mesa—pequeña,* | The house is big, the table—small, |
| *la puerta—cerrada, la ventana abierta.* | the door—closed, the window—open. |

## Papa Chant

*Yo como una papa, no como a mi papá.*
    I eat a potato, I don't eat my dad.
*Una papa es comida, un papá es un padre.*
    A *papa* is a potato, a *papá* is a father.

*Due to differences in languages, literal translations of chants may lose meaning and/or the sense of rhythm.

# Introductions and Greetings

¡Hola!

¿Cómo te llamas?

Me llamo _____.

¡Adiós!

¿Cómo estás?

bien

**55** *Spanish: Grade 2*

This page is intentionally left blank.

# Introductions and Greetings

mal

así, así

¿Cuántos años tienes?

Tengo _____ años.

✓

sí

⊘

no

This page is intentionally left blank.

# Introductions and Greetings

por favor

gracias

amigo

amiga

amigos

¡Hasta luego!

**59** *Spanish: Grade 2*

This page is intentionally left blank.

*Spanish: Grade 2*

# Animals

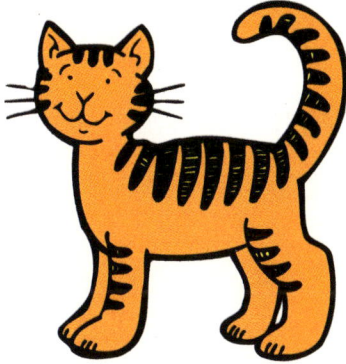

gato

perro

pájaro

pez

pato

culebra

This page is intentionally left blank.

# Clothing

camisa

pantalones

vestido

calcetines

zapatos

gorro

This page is intentionally left blank.

# Clothing

chaqueta

pantalones cortos

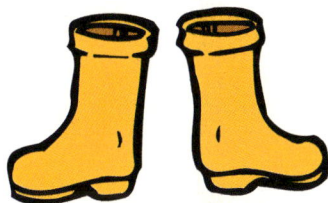

botas

guantes

falda

abrigo

 *Spanish: Grade 2*

This page is intentionally left blank.

# Community

escuela

tienda

museo

biblioteca

casa

parque

This page is intentionally left blank.

# Classroom Objects

silla

mesa

tijeras

libro

lápiz

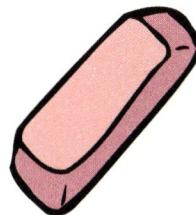

borrador

This page is intentionally left blank.

# Classroom Objects

ventana

cuaderno

papel

puerta

pluma

escritorio

**71**     *Spanish: Grade 2*

This page is intentionally left blank.

## Numbers 0–10

Trace, then write each of the number words from 0 to 10 in Spanish.
Use the words at the left to help you.

| | | | | | |
|---|---|---|---|---|---|
| 0 | cero | cero | cero | cero | cero |
| 1 | uno | uno | uno | uno | uno |
| 2 | dos | dos | dos | dos | dos |
| 3 | tres | tres | tres | tres | tres |
| 4 | cuatro | cuatro | cuatro | | cuatro |
| 5 | cinco | cinco | cinco | cinco | cinco |
| 6 | seis | seis | seis | seis | seis |
| 7 | siete | siete | siete | siete | siete |
| 8 | ocho | ocho | ocho | ocho | ocho |
| 9 | nueve | nueve | nueve | | nueve |
| 10 | diez | diez | diez | diez | diez |

**4**

## Numbers 0–10

Say each word out loud. Circle the number that tells the meaning of
the word.

| | | | |
|---|---|---|---|
| seis | 5 | 0 | (6) |
| ocho | 1 | 9 | (8) |
| uno | 3 | (1) | 8 |
| cero | 8 | 10 | (0) |
| siete | 9 | (7) | 1 |
| tres | 0 | (3) | 5 |
| diez | (10) | 8 | 7 |
| nueve | 4 | 2 | (9) |
| cuatro | 7 | 5 | (4) |
| dos | (2) | 6 | 3 |
| cinco | 6 | 4 | (5) |

**5**

## Dot-to-Dot

Connect the dots. Start with the Spanish word for one and stop at ten. What shape
did you get? _____

**6**

## Numbers 0–20

In the left column, write the number words from 0 to 10 in Spanish. Use the words
in the box below to help you. Then, in the second column, write the numbers beside
each Spanish word. Examples are done for you.

| | | | |
|---|---|---|---|
| 0 | cero | 11 | once |
| 1 | uno | 12 | doce |
| 2 | dos | 13 | trece |
| 3 | tres | 14 | catorce |
| 4 | cuatro | 15 | quince |
| 5 | cinco | 16 | dieciséis |
| 6 | seis | 17 | diecisiete |
| 7 | siete | 18 | dieciocho |
| 8 | ocho | 19 | diecinueve |
| 9 | nueve | 20 | veinte |
| 10 | diez | | |

siete   ocho   uno   seis   nueve
cero   cinco   dos   cuatro   diez   tres

Now, count from 1 to 20 in Spanish. Point to the numbers as you say them.

① ② ③ ④ ⑤ ⑥ ⑦ ⑧ ⑨ ⑩
⑪ ⑫ ⑬ ⑭ ⑮ ⑯ ⑰ ⑱ ⑲ ⑳

**7**

## Show Your Numbers

In each box, write the number for the word written. Then, draw
and color pictures that show the numbers.

| | | |
|---|---|---|
| dieciséis means 16 | trece means 13 | ocho means 8 |
| catorce means 14 | seis means 6 | once means 11 |
| *Pictures Will Vary.* | | |
| dos means 2 | veinte means 20 | cinco means 5 |
| doce means 12 | diez means 10 | quince means 15 |

**8**

## Sunshine 0–20

Write the number for each Spanish word. Cross out the correct number of suns to
show the number written in Spanish. The first is done for you.

| | | |
|---|---|---|
| quince 15 | veinte 20 | tres 3 |
| once 11 | nueve 9 | trece 13 |
| catorce 14 | dieciocho 18 | cero 0 |
| doce 12 — **My favorite number** *Answers Will Vary.* | | seis 6 |

**9**

# Number Puzzle

Write the English number words in the puzzle spaces. Follow the Spanish clues.

**Word Bank**

| | | | |
|---|---|---|---|
| one | eight | eleven | seventeen |
| two | nine | thirteen | eighteen |
| six | ten | fourteen | twenty |

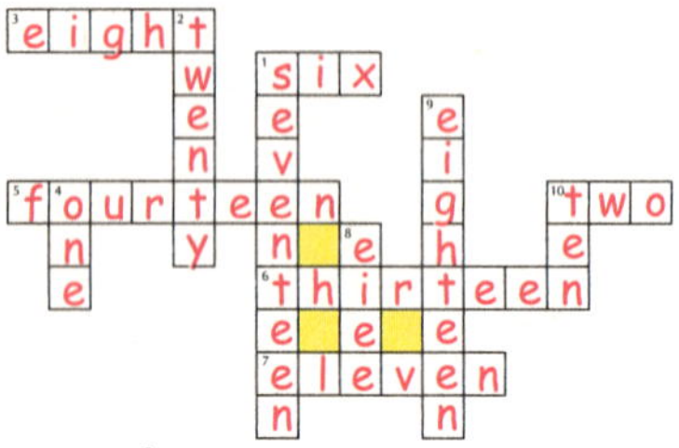


**Down**

1. diecisiete
2. veinte
4. uno
8. nueve
9. dieciocho
10. diez

**Across**

1. seis
3. ocho
5. catorce
6. trece
7. once
10. dos

**10**

# Counting On

Follow a pattern to write the numbers from 21–29. Change *veinte* (20) to *veinti* and add the number words from *uno* to *nueve*. (Watch for accent marks on *dos, tres,* and *seis.*)

Rewrite the number words in the Word Bank in order.

**Word Bank**

veintiséis, veinticinco, treinta, veintiocho, veintidós, veintiuno, veintinueve, veinticuatro, veintisiete, veintitrés

| | | | |
|---|---|---|---|
| 21 | veintiuno | 26 | veintiséis |
| 22 | veintidós | 27 | veintisiete |
| 23 | veintitrés | 28 | veintiocho |
| 24 | veinticuatro | 29 | veintinueve |
| 25 | veinticinco | 30 | trienta |

Complete the pattern to write the numbers from 31–39. Use the word *y* to join *treinta* (30) with the number words *uno* to *nueve*.

| | | | |
|---|---|---|---|
| 30 | treinta | 35 | treinta y cinco |
| 31 | treinta y uno | 36 | treinta y seis |
| 32 | treinta y dos | 37 | treinta y siete |
| 33 | treinta y tres | 38 | treinta y ocho |
| 34 | treinta y cuatro | 39 | treinta y nueve |

**11**

# The Alphabet

**El abecedario (the alphabet)**

| | | | | | |
|---|---|---|---|---|---|
| **a** | a | **k** | ka | **s** | ese |
| **b** | be | **l** | ele | **t** | te |
| **c** | ce | **m** | eme | **u** | u |
| **d** | de | **n** | ene | **v** | ve |
| **e** | e | **ñ** | eñe | **w** | doble ve |
| **f** | efe | **o** | o | **x** | equis |
| **g** | ge | **p** | pe | **y** | i griega |
| **h** | hache | **q** | cu | **z** | zeta |
| **i** | i | **r** | ere | | |
| **j** | jota | **rr** | erre | | |

**Listening Practice**

Write the Spanish word for each number below. Then, spell each word out loud.

| | | | | | | | |
|---|---|---|---|---|---|---|---|
| 1 | uno | 5 | cinco | 9 | nueve | 13 | trece |
| 2 | dos | 6 | seis | 10 | diez | 14 | catorce |
| 3 | tres | 7 | siete | 11 | once | 15 | quince |
| 4 | cuatro | 8 | ocho | 12 | doce | 16 | dieciséis |

**12**

# Using You

Spanish uses two different forms of the pronoun *you*.

**tú**

***Tú*** is used when talking to

1. someone you refer to by a first name.
2. your sister, brother, or cousin.
3. a classmate.
4. a close friend.
5. a child younger than yourself.

**usted**

***Usted*** **(*Ud.*)** is used when talking to

1. someone with a title.
2. an older person.
3. a stranger.
4. a person of authority.

Write the names of 6 or more people in each box below.

| Use **tú** when you are talking to . . . | Use **usted** when you are talking to . . . |
|---|---|
| Answers Will Vary. | |

**13**

# Picking Pronouns

Spanish uses two different forms of the pronoun *you*.

**tú**

***Tú*** is used when talking to

1. someone you refer to by a first name.
2. your sister, brother, or cousin.
3. a classmate.
4. a close friend.
5. a child younger than yourself.

**usted**

***Usted*** **(*Ud.*)** is used when talking to

1. someone with a title.
2. an older person.
3. a stranger.
4. a person of authority.

Explain to whom you might be talking and what you are asking in each question.

¿Cómo te llamas tú? Asking someone your own age or younger what his/her name is.

¿Cómo se llama usted? Asking someone older or a person of authority what his/her name is.

¿Cómo estás tú? Asking someone your own age or younger how he/she is.

¿Cómo está usted? Asking someone older or a person of authority how he/she is.

¿Cuántos años tienes tú? Asking someone your own age or younger how old he/she is.

¿Cuántos años tiene usted? Asking someone older or a person with authority how old he/she is.

**14**

# More Than One

Spanish nouns can be placed into two groups—singular nouns (one of something) or plural nouns (more than one of something). Nouns that end in *–s* are usually plural. Nouns ending in other letters are usually singular.

Read the following familiar nouns. Write **S** if the noun is singular and **P** if the noun is plural.

| | | |
|---|---|---|
| P 1. calcetines | S 2. dedo | P 3. botas |
| S 4. cuerpo | P 5. vegetales | S 6. ciudad |
| S 7. escuela | P 8. sandalias | P 9. zapatos |
| P 10. guantes | S 11. casa | S 12. boca |

Follow these rules to write the following Spanish words in the plural.

1. If the word ends in a vowel, add *-s.*
2. If the word ends in a consonant, add *-es.*
3. If the word ends in *z,* change the *z* to *c* before adding *-es.*

| | | | |
|---|---|---|---|
| 1. carne | carnes | 6. nariz | narices |
| 2. silla | sillas | 7. abrigo | abrigos |
| 3. ciudad | ciudades | 8. señor | señores |
| 4. lápiz | lápices | 9. borrador | borradores |
| 5. azul | azules | 10. pollo | pollos |

**15**

## More and More

Write the plural form of each Spanish clue word in the puzzle.

Crossword puzzle answers:
- hombros
- borrador
- vasos
- faldas
- zapatos
- museos
- escuelas
- narices
- gatos
- sombreros
- casas
- osos
- mesas
- lápices

**Across**

1. hombro
4. falda
5. zapato
7. museo
8. nariz
10. gato
11. sombrero
13. oso
14. lápiz

**Down**

2. borrador
3. vaso
6. escuela
9. casa
12. mesa

**16**

---

## First Sentences

Create original sentences in Spanish using these sentence starters and the verbs in the Word Bank. You may use one sentence starter more than once. Write the English meanings on the lines below the Spanish.

### Word Bank

| comer | beber | dormir | tocar |
|-------|-------|--------|-------|
| hablar | limpiar | mirar | dar |

### Sentence Starters

| Me gusta _____ . | (I like _____ .) |
|---|---|
| No me gusta _____ . | (I don't like _____ .) |
| Quiero _____ . | (I want _____ .) |
| Necesito _____ . | (I need _____ .) |

1. _____
2. _____
3. _____   *Sentences Will Vary.*
4. _____
5. _____

**17**

---

## Action Words

Refer to the Word Bank to write the Spanish word that matches each picture.

| Word Bank | comer | estudiar | limpiar | mirar | jugar | dar |
|-----------|-------|----------|---------|-------|-------|-----|
| | hablar | beber | dormir | trabajar | tocar | ir |

- to clean — limpiar
- to touch — tocar
- to eat — comer
- to speak — hablar
- to watch — mirar
- to drink — beber
- to give — dar
- to sleep — dormir
- to study — estudiar
- to go — ir
- to work — trabajar
- to play — jugar

**18**

---

## Capitals

Spanish uses capital letters less often than the English language. Follow these rules as your guide.

### Capitalization Rules

1. All Spanish sentences begin with capital letters.
2. Names of people begin with capital letters.
3. Names of places (cities, regions, countries, continents) and holidays begin with capital letters.
4. Titles are not capitalized unless abbreviated (señor–Sr., usted–Ud.).
5. Some words that are normally capitalized in English may not be capitalized in Spanish (nationalities, religions, languages, months, and days).

Write *sí* if the word should be capitalized. Write *no* if it should remain lowercase.

1. sarah — sí
2. inglés — no
3. navidad — sí
4. español — no
5. mexicano — no
6. africa — sí
7. señor — no
8. enero — no
9. domingo — no
10. católico — no
11. santa fé — sí
12. viernes — no
13. méxico — sí
14. julio — no
15. colorado — sí
16. miguel — sí

**19**

---

## Categories

Read the list of words given. Write the words in the proper columns. If the word needs a capital letter, write it that way.

los angeles, maría, uds., inglés, san diego, señorita, españa, susana, sr., sra., viernes, cuba, ustedes, san antonio, santa fé, oceano pacífico, juan, septiembre, americano, américa del norte, español, señora, josé, mexicano, lunes, méxico, católico, señor

| People | Places | Titles | Not Capitalized |
|--------|--------|--------|-----------------|
| María | Los Angeles | Uds. | inglés |
| Susana | San Diego | Sr. | señorita |
| Juan | España | Sra. | viernes |
| José | Cuba | | ustedes |
| | San Antonio | | septiembre |
| | Santa Fé | | americano |
| | Océano Pacífica | | español |
| | América del Norte | | señora |
| | México | | mexicana |
| | | | lunes |
| | | | católico |
| | | | señor |

**20**

---

## Introductions

Say each expression out loud. Circle the picture that tells the meaning of each word.

- gracias
- Tengo seis años.
- por favor
- amigo
- amigos
- ¡Hasta luego!
- amiga
- sí

**22**

---

## Puzzle of the Week

Write the Spanish words in the puzzle.

**Across**
2. Thursday
7. Wednesday

**Down**
1. Monday
3. Saturday
4. Friday
5. Sunday
6. Tuesday

**Word Bank**

| | | |
|---|---|---|
| jueves | domingo | martes |
| sábado | viernes | lunes |
| | miércoles | |

**23**

## Spanish Months

Write the Spanish word for the clue words in the crossword puzzle.

**Across**
4. July
9. May
10. September
11. June
12. January

**Down**
1. April
2. November
3. December
5. March
6. February
7. August
8. October

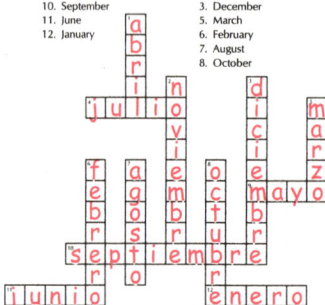

**Word Bank**

| | | |
|---|---|---|
| marzo | mayo | junio |
| septiembre | octubre | julio |
| abril | enero | febrero | noviembre |

**24**

## Pictures to Color

Color the pictures according to each color word.

| rojo | azul |
|---|---|
| verde | anaranjado |
| morado | amarillo |

**25**

## Rainbow Colors

Color the picture according to the color words shown.

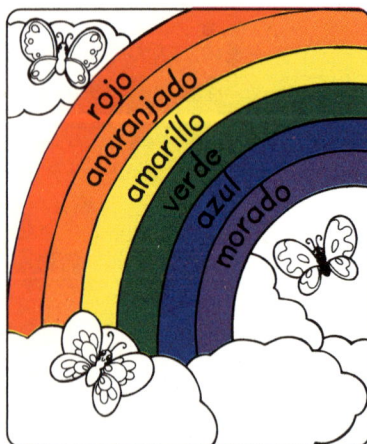

rojo
anaranjado
amarillo
verde
azul
morado

**26**

## Color the Cars

Color the cars according to the color words shown.

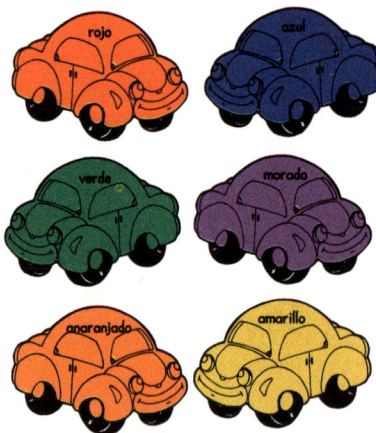

rojo   azul
verde   morado
anaranjado   amarillo

**27**

## Color Copy

Copy the following words in the color of each word.
Which word is hard to see with the actual color? blanco (white)

| rojo | rojo |
| azul | azul |
| verde | verde |
| anaranjado | anaranjado |
| morado | morado |
| amarillo | amarillo |
| café | cafe |
| negro | negro |
| blanco | blanco |
| rosado | rosado |

**28**

## Food Meanings

Say each word out loud. Circle the picture that shows the meaning of each word.

| papa | | potato |
| ensalada | salad | cheese |
| queso | cheese | drumstick |
| pan | potato | bread |
| leche | milk | grape juice |
| pollo | drumstick | bread |
| jugo | salad | grape juice |

**29**

## Mixed-Up Food

Draw a line from the word to the food picture.

papa
ensalada
queso
pan
leche
jugo
pollo

**30**

## Food Words

Say each word out loud. Copy each word and color the picture.

sopa — sopa
agua — agua
naranja — naranja
carne — carne

Colors Will Vary.

plátano — plátano
manzana — manzana
sandwich — sandwich

**31**

## Animals All Around

Copy each word and color the pictures.

perro — perro
gato — gato
pájaro — pájaro

Colors Will Vary.

pez — pez
pato — pato
culebra — culebra

**32**

## Animal Art

Choose four animals and draw each animal in its home. Label it with the Spanish animal word.

Animals Will Vary.

**33**

## Clothing

Say each word out loud. Copy each word and color the picture.

pantalones — pantalones
gorro — gorro
vestido — vestido

camisa — camisa
calcetines — calcetines
zapatos — zapatos

**34**

## Clothing

Say each word out loud. Copy each word and color the picture.

abrigo
▶ abrigo
chaqueta
▶ chaqueta
falda
▶ falda

▶ guantes
guantes
▶ pantalones cortos
pantalones cortos
▶ botas
botas

**35**

## Remember These?

Fill in the blanks with the missing letters. Use the Spanish clothing words at the bottom to help you.

c a m i s a
f a l d a   a b r i g o
z a p a t o s   g o r r o   b o t a s
p a n t a l o n e s
v e s t i d o

| camisa | vestido | pantalones | falda |
| zapatos | gorro | abrigo | botas |

**36**

## What Belongs?

Circle the item that does not belong with the other two. Write its name in Spanish below its picture.

gorro

guantes

pantalones

Circle the two items that are alike. Say the item in Spanish that is not like the other two. Color the pictures.

Colors Will Vary.

**37**

## Head to Toe

Using the Word Banks, label the parts of the face and body.

nariz
ojos
orejas
cara
tientes
pelo
boca

**Word Bank**
cara   ojos   boca   nariz   dientes   orejas   pelo

hombro
mano
dedo
cabeza
erpo
estómago
rodilla
dedo
brazo
pie
pierna

**Word Bank**
cuerpo   cabeza   mano   pierna   hombro
brazo   dedo   pie   rodilla   estómago

**38**

## Head and Shoulders

Refer to the Word Bank to label each body part in Spanish.

cabeza
hombro
braza
cuerpo
estómago
mano
rodilla
pierna
dedo
pie

**Word Bank**
cuerpo   pie
brazo   pierna
cabeza   rodilla
dedo   hombro
mano   estómago

**39**

## Knees and Toes

Write the Spanish words for the clues in the crossword puzzle.

**Word Bank**
cuerpo   cabeza   mano   pierna   hombro
brazo   dedo   pie   rodilla   estómago

**Across**
2. foot
3. body
5. knee
6. head
7. shoulder
9. hand

**Down**
1. finger or toe
2. leg
4. stomach
8. arm

dedo   pie
cuerpo   pierna
estomago
rodilla
cabeza
hombro
brazo
mano

**40**

## Family Word Meanings

Say each word out loud. Circle the picture that shows the meaning of each word.

padre

chica

abuela

madre

abuelo

chico

**41**

## Family

Copy each word and color the pictures.

madre
> madre

padre
> padre

abuelo
> abuelo

abuela
> abuela

chica
> chica

chico
> chico

Colors Will Vary.

Let's learn two new words:

hermano
> hermano

hermana
> hermana

**42**

## Family Crossword

Use the Spanish words at the bottom of the page to fill in your answers.

```
        h e r m a n a
p a d r e   b   b
      r     u   u
      m a d r e l
      a     l   o
c h i c a
c h i c o
```

**ACROSS**
1. sister
4. father
5. mother
6. girl
7. boy

**DOWN**
1. brother
2. grandmother
3. grandfather

| padre | madre |
| chico | chica |
| abuelo | abuela |
| hermano | hermana |

**43**

## Listen Well

Say each word out loud. Circle the picture for each Spanish word.

| padre | | | |
| abuelo | | | |
| hermana | | | |
| chica | | | |
| abuela | | | |
| madre | | | |
| hermano | | | |
| chico | | | |

**44**

## Picture This

Say each word out loud. Circle the picture that shows the meaning of each word.

casa

escuela

tienda

parque

biblioteca

museo

**45**

## My Neighborhood

Draw a picture of an imaginary neighborhood. Add streets, trees, and whatever else you wish to make your neighborhood look nice. Color your picture.

Mi barrio

Pictures Will Vary.

Label your neighborhood with the words you learned.

casa   parque   biblioteca   tienda   escuela   museo

**46**

## Places to Go

Say each word out loud. Copy each word and color the picture.

museo

escuela
▶ museo
casa

▶ escuela
▶ casa

Dinosaurios

Colors Will Vary.

FOOD-MART

▶ tienda
▶ parque

tienda
parque

▶ biblioteca

biblioteca

**47**

## Place Words

Fill in the blanks for place words. Use the Spanish words at the bottom to help you.

FOOD-MART

House    CASA

t
b i b l i o t e c a
e          s
n        m u s e o
d          c
p a r q u e   u
e
c a s a
l
a

| escuela | museo | casa |
| biblioteca | tienda | parque |

**48**

## Classroom Things

Copy each word and color the picture.

mesa

silla
▶ mesa
lápiz

▶ silla
▶ lápiz

Colors Will Vary.

▶ tijeras
▶ libro

tijeras
libro

▶ borrador

borrador

**49**

## Classroom Words

Say each word out loud. Copy each word and color the picture.

cuaderno

ventana
▶ cuaderno
puerta

▶ ventana
▶ puerta

Colors Will Vary.

▶ pluma
▶ papel

pluma
papel

▶ escritorio

escritorio

**50**

## Listen Carefully

Say each word out loud. Circle the picture that tells the meaning of each word.

libro

tijeras

ventana

silla

pluma

lápiz

cuaderno

mesa

puerta

**51**